Snakehead

Super Sleuth

Star Pilot

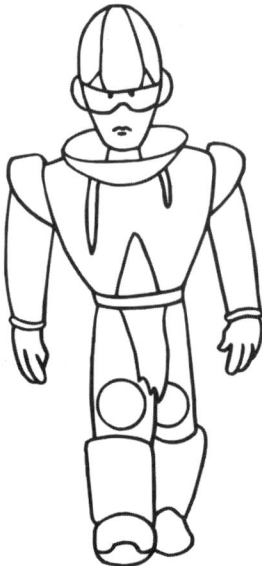

Super Bug

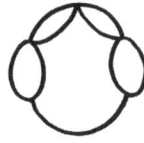

Robo

Kango Kicker

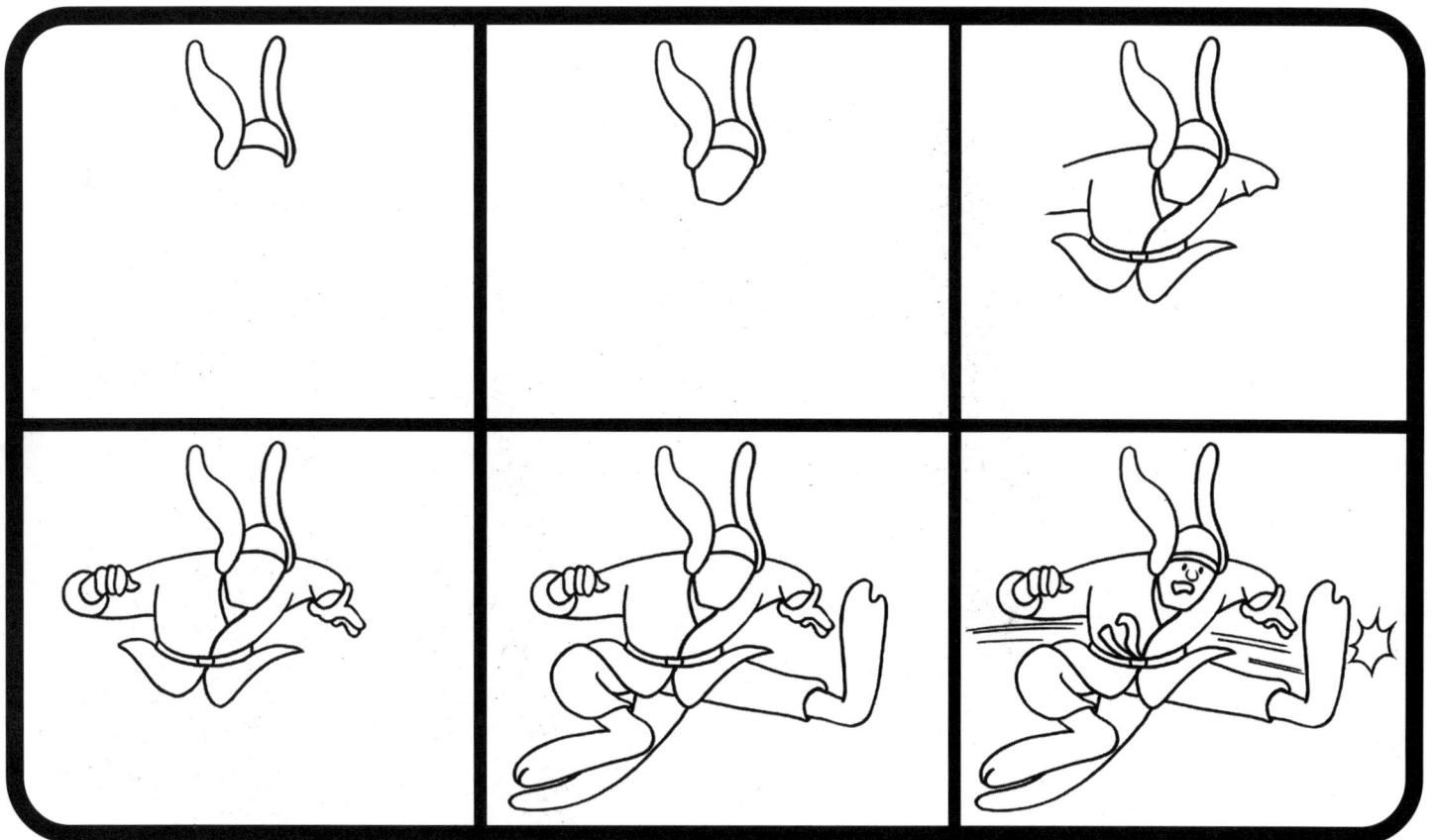

Greek Hero

Sky Scraper

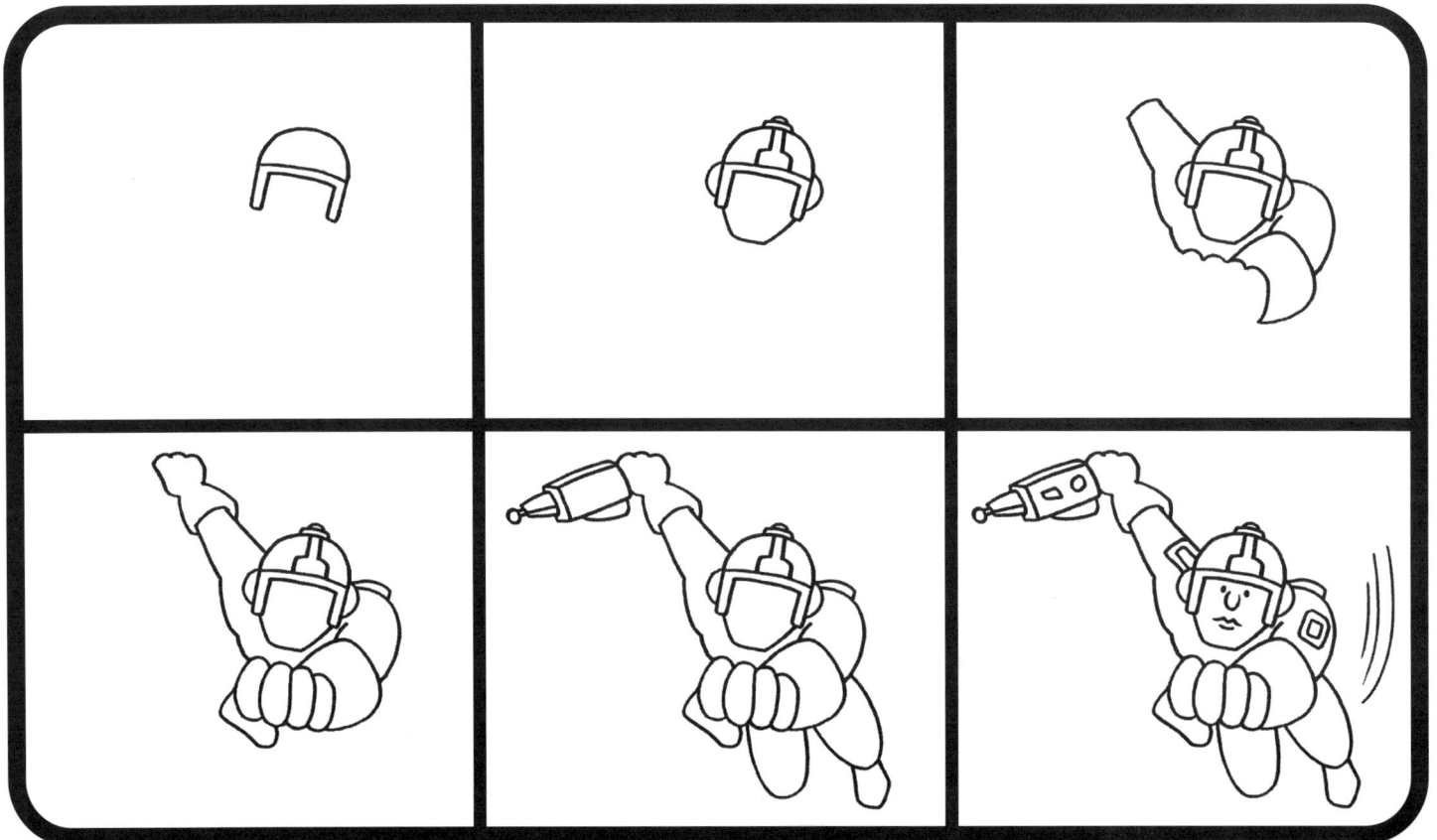

G.I.

Markovian Lancer

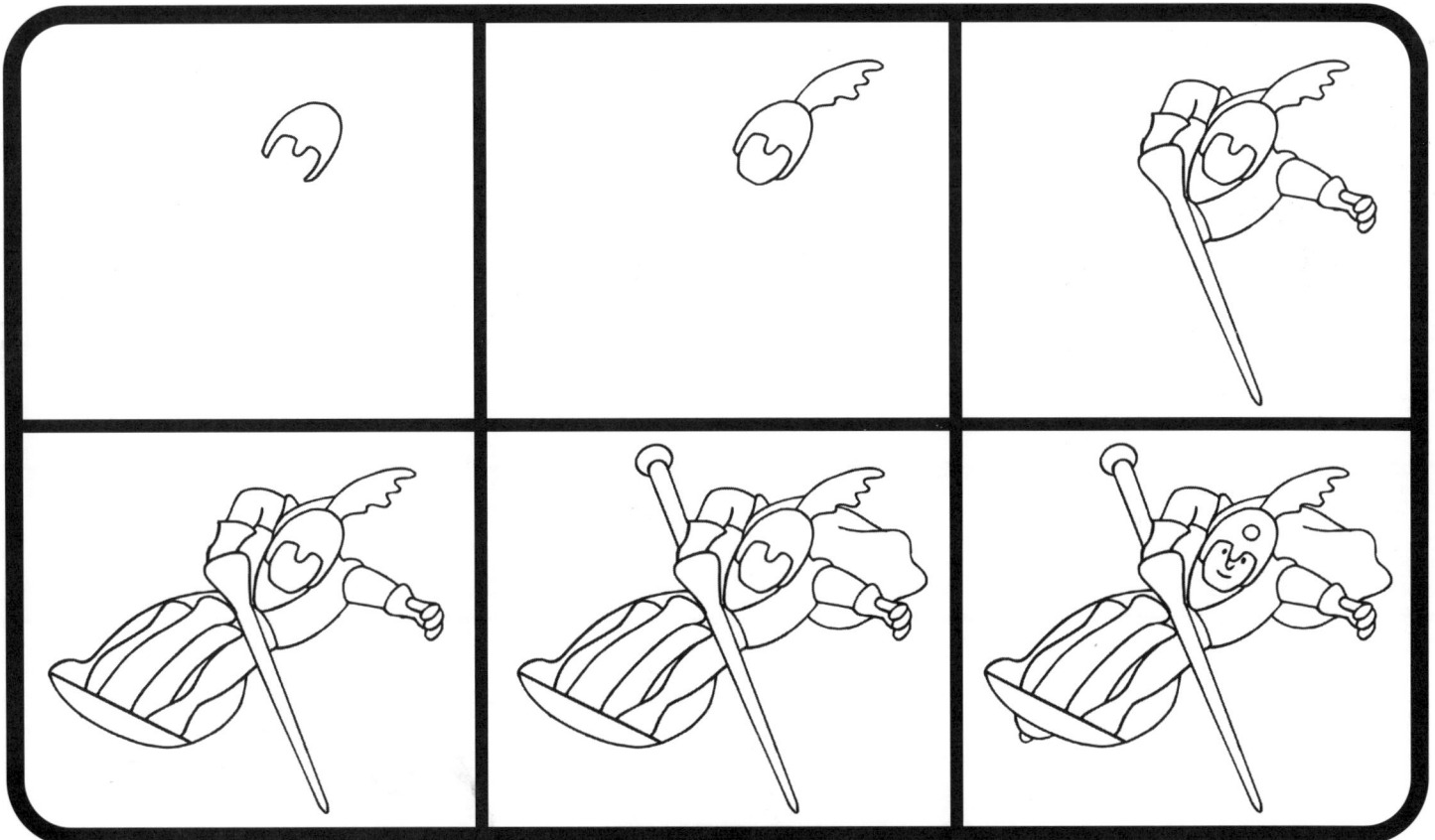

Space Queen

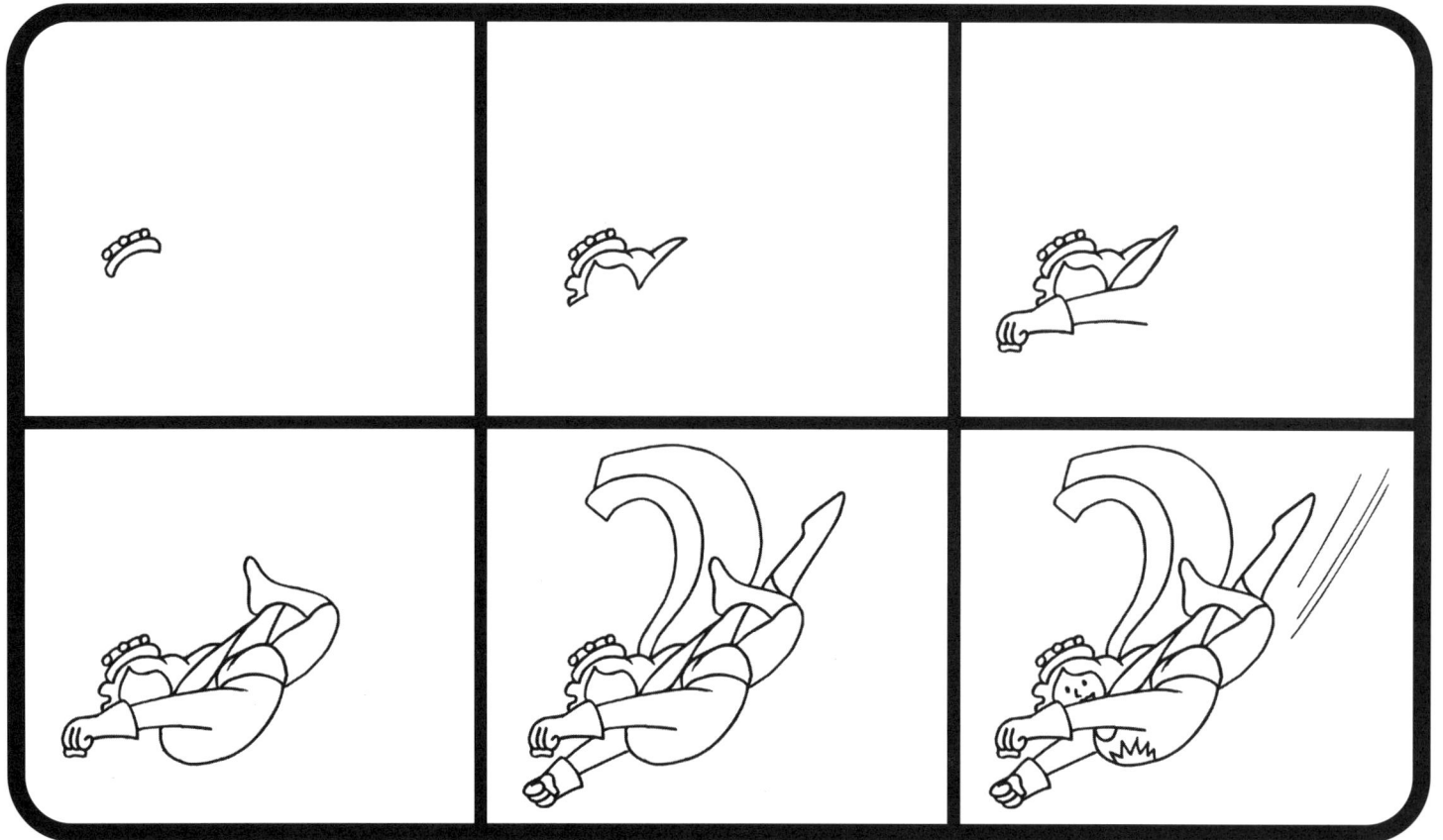

Super Charger

Super Egor

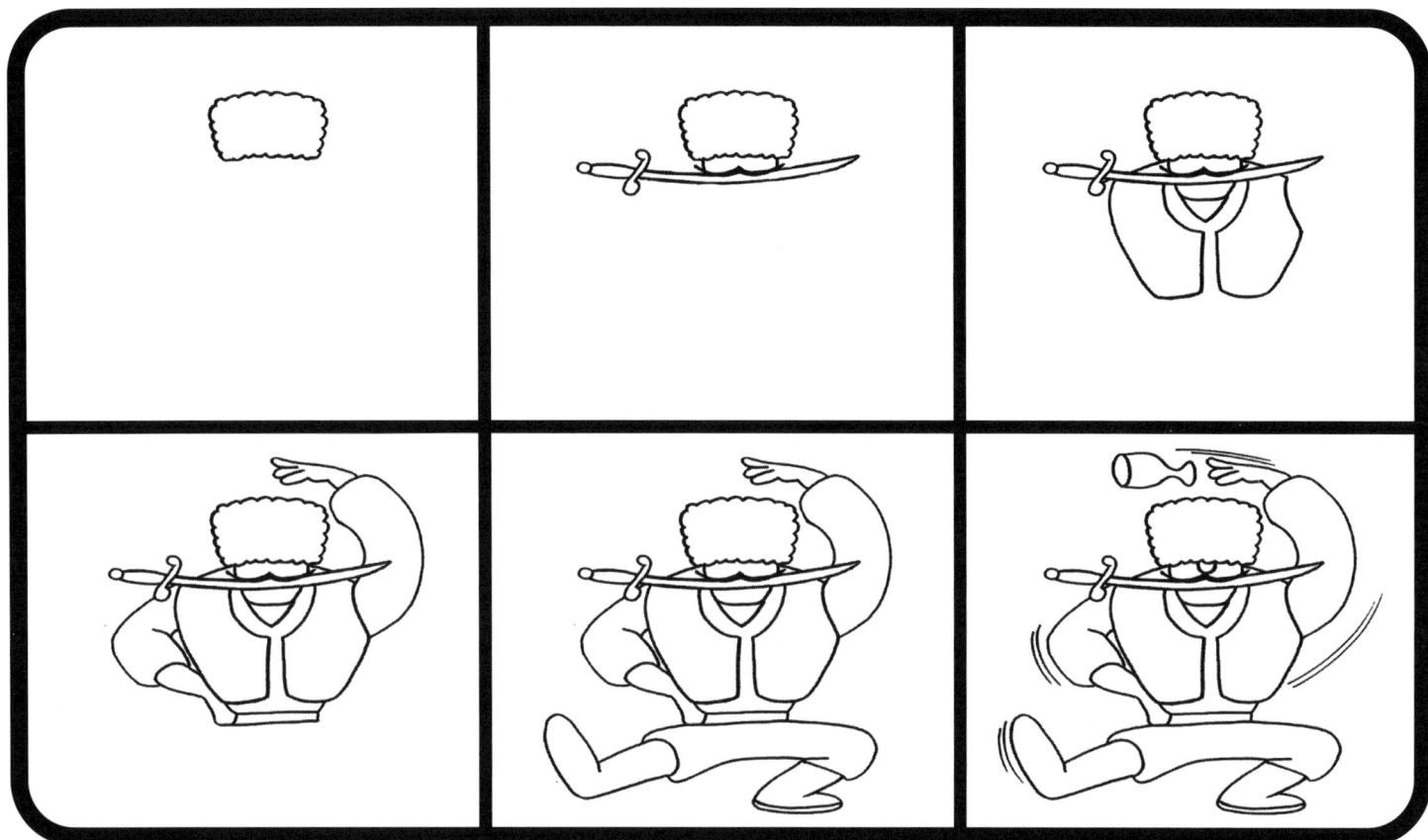

Skater

Lizardus

Surf Boarder

Swash Buccaneer

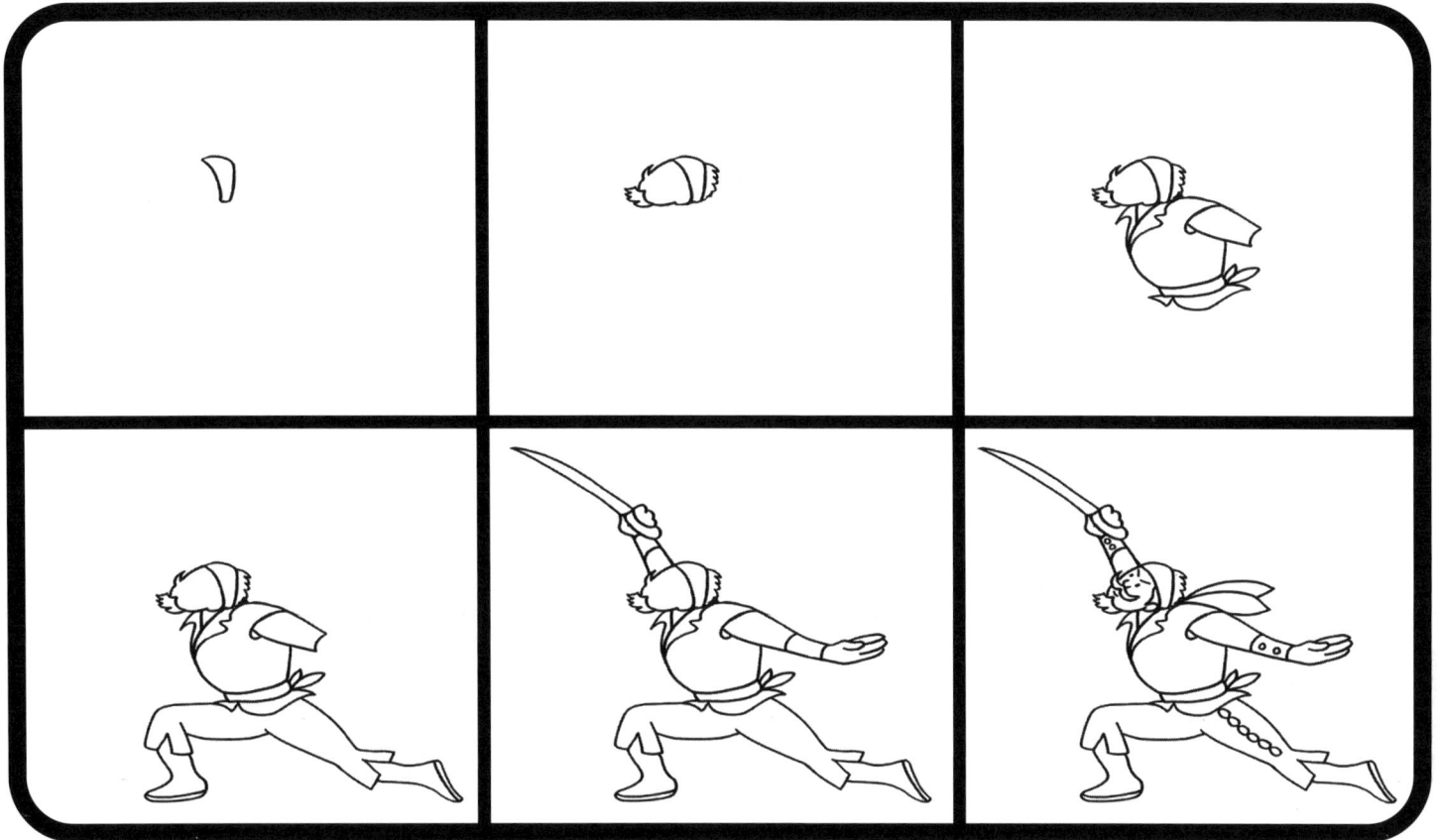

Space Skater

Super Star

Sky Leaper

Queen Boudicca

Aztec

Super Saver

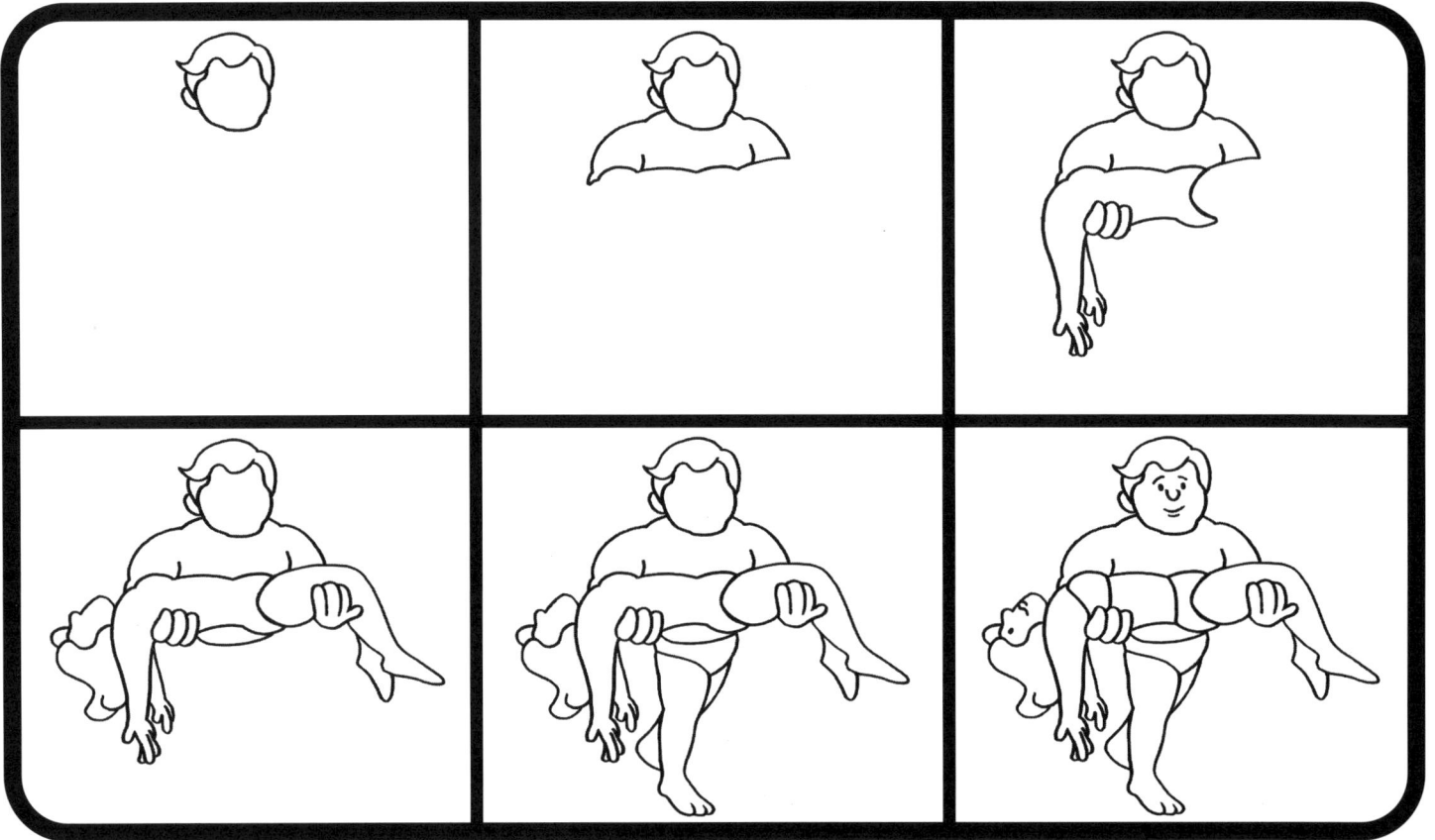

Samurai

Karate King

Sky Diver

Space Sniper

Prince Sword

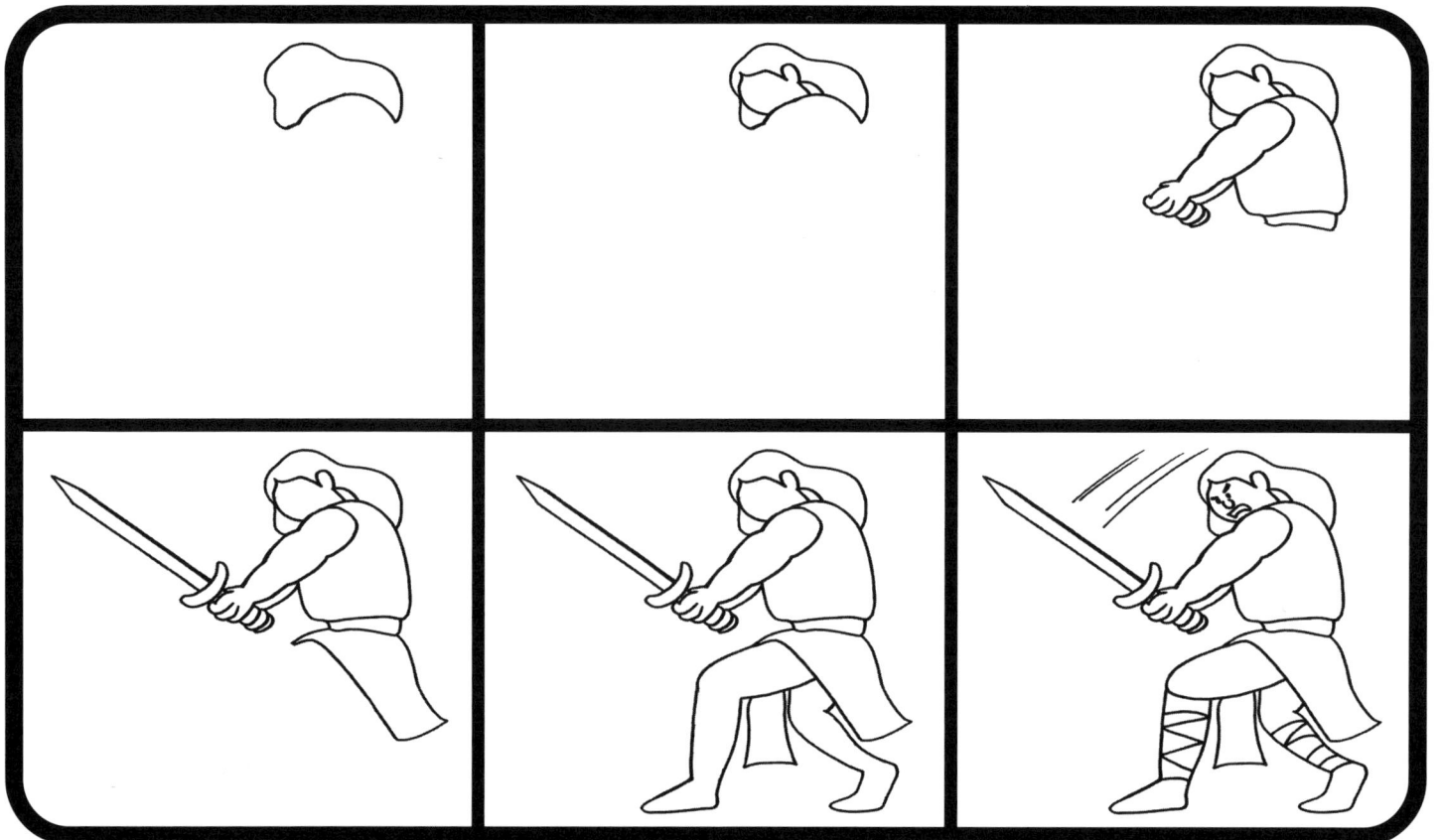

Robot Warrior

Frogman

Kajo

Zulu

Star Hunter

Space Shield

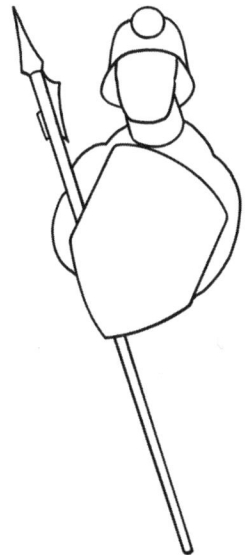
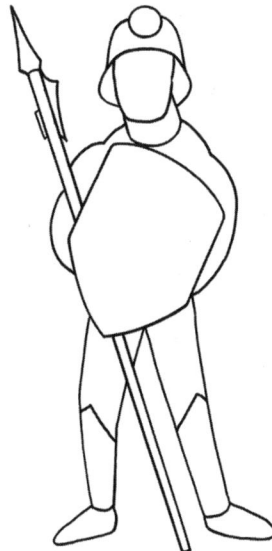

Star Warden

Spartacus

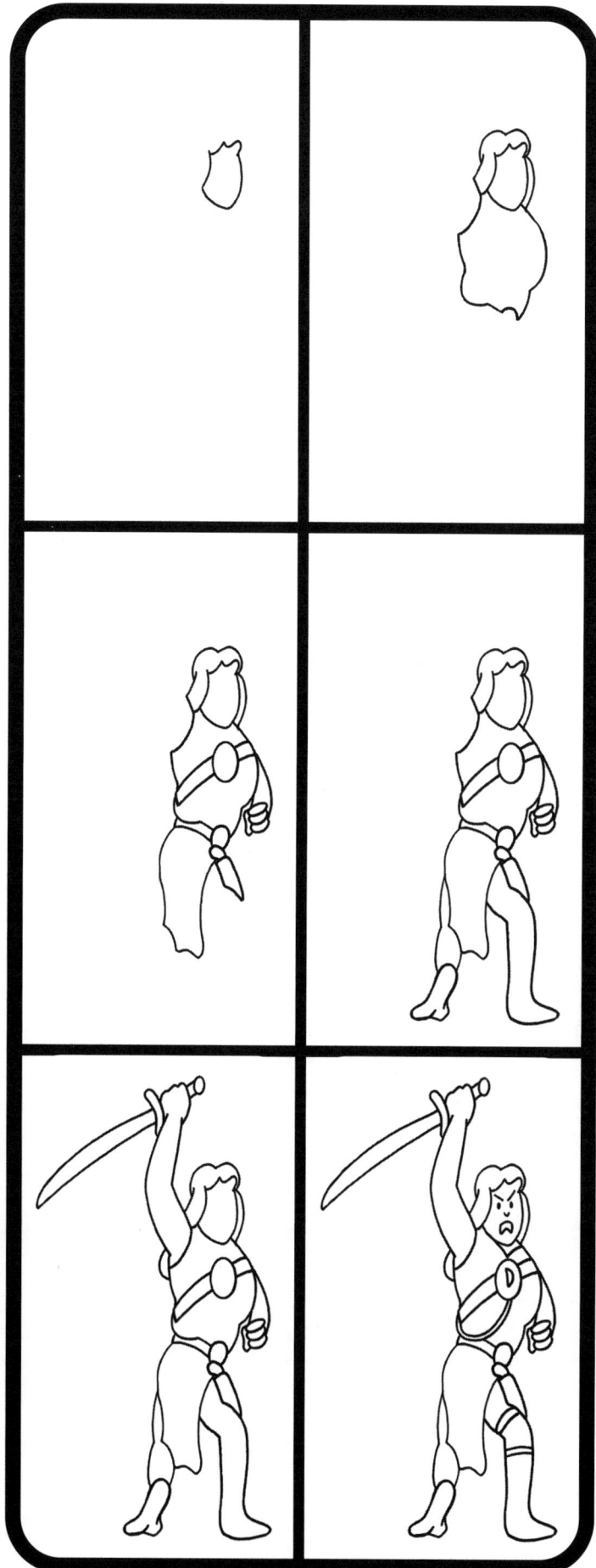

Sky Boxer

Venus Amazon

The Archer

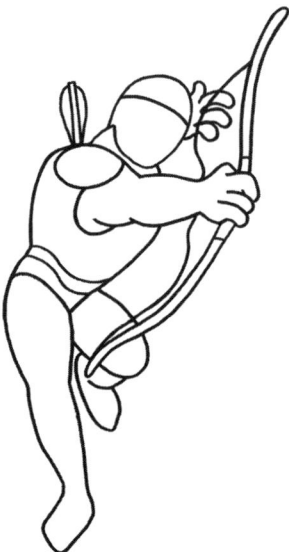

Lightning

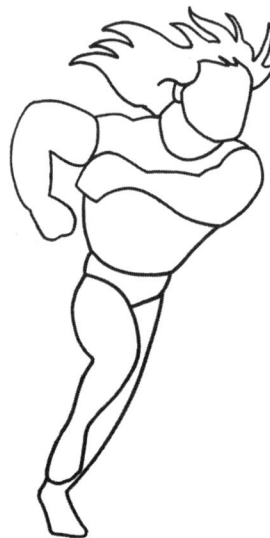

Ninja

Axeman

UDDz

Captain Galactic

Demon Slayer

Lightning Diver

Mechanic Man

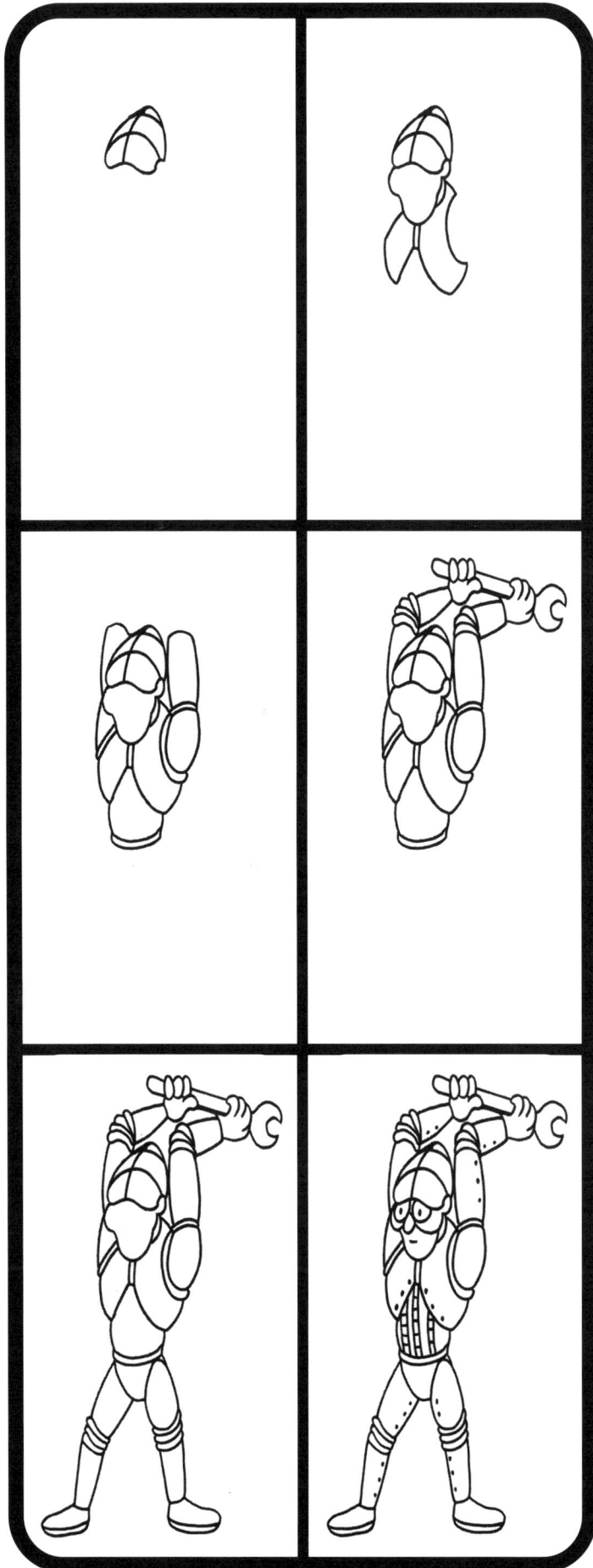

Demon Fighter

Space Warrior

Sonic Hero

Space Robot

Space Baroness

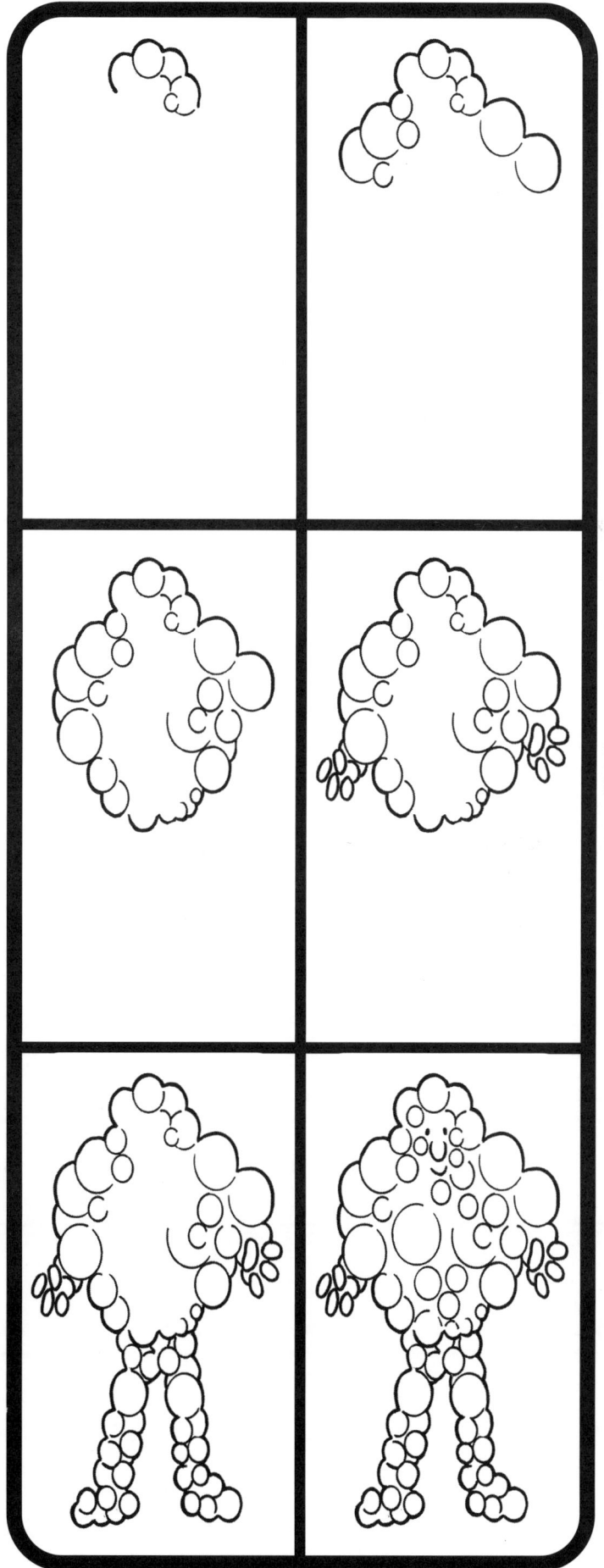

The Bat

Globe Man

Super oil

Rope Breaker

Buffalo Bill

Galactica

Super Moose

Volgan

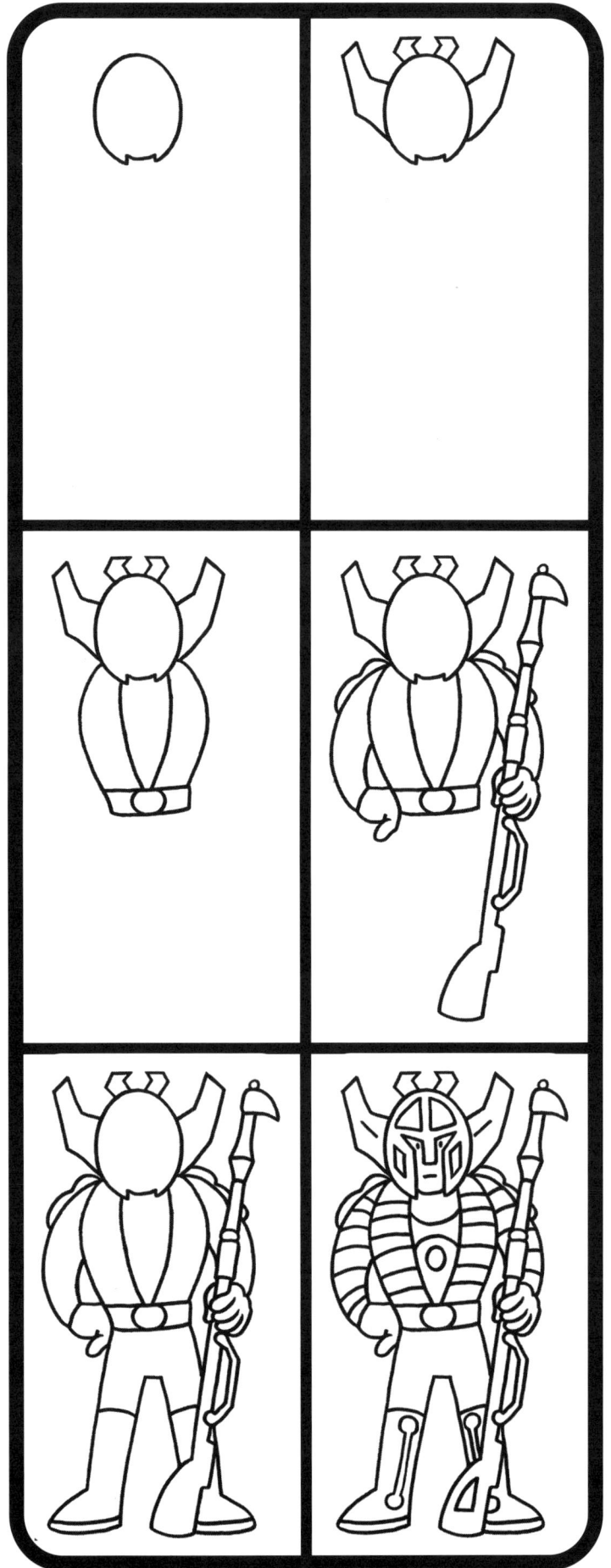

Super Duck

Hammer Head

Sir-Lance-A-Lot

Hannibal

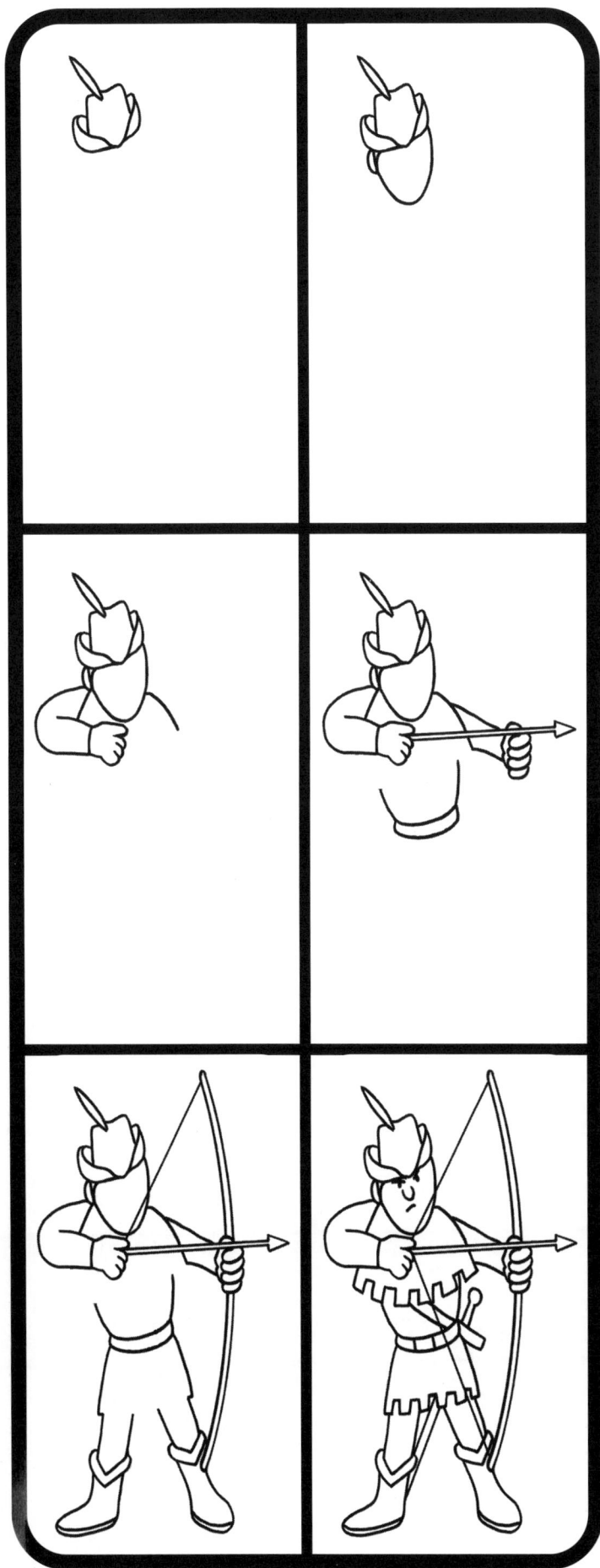

Robin Hood

Dragon Queen

Super Mum

Jungle Man

Blade Warrior

Celtic Warrior

Super Thor

Super caveman

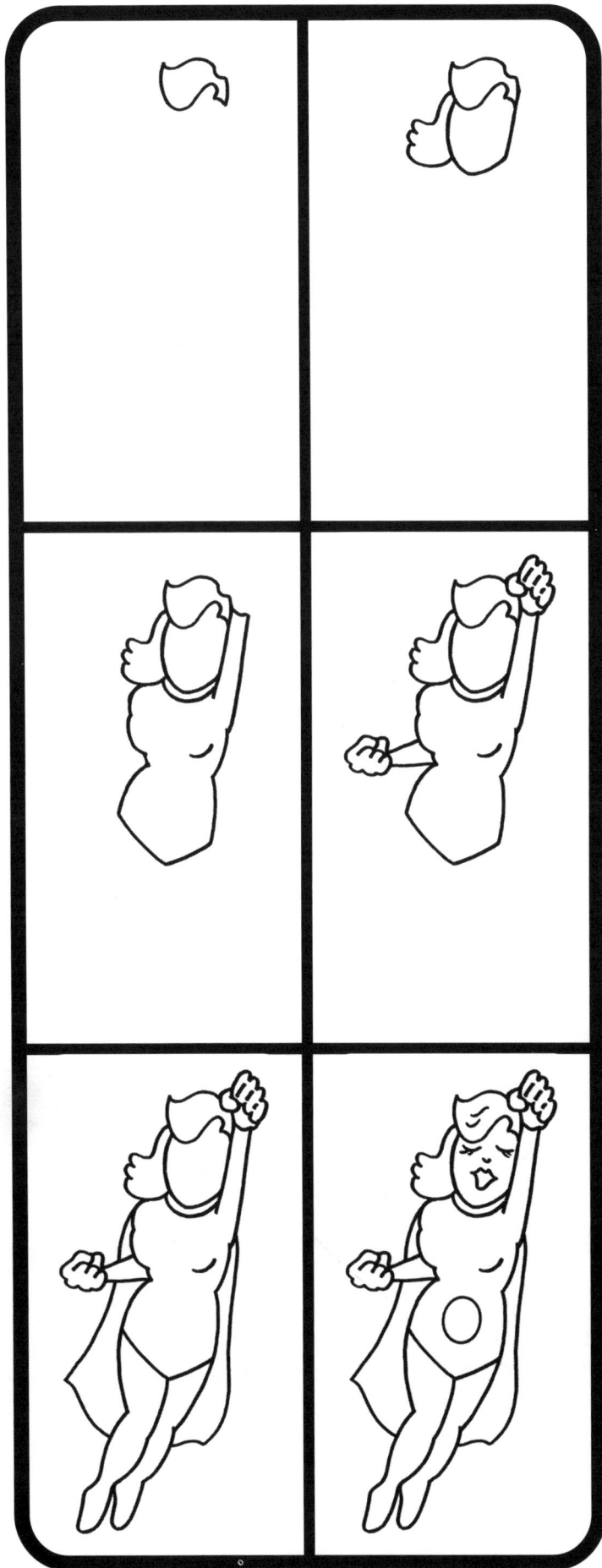

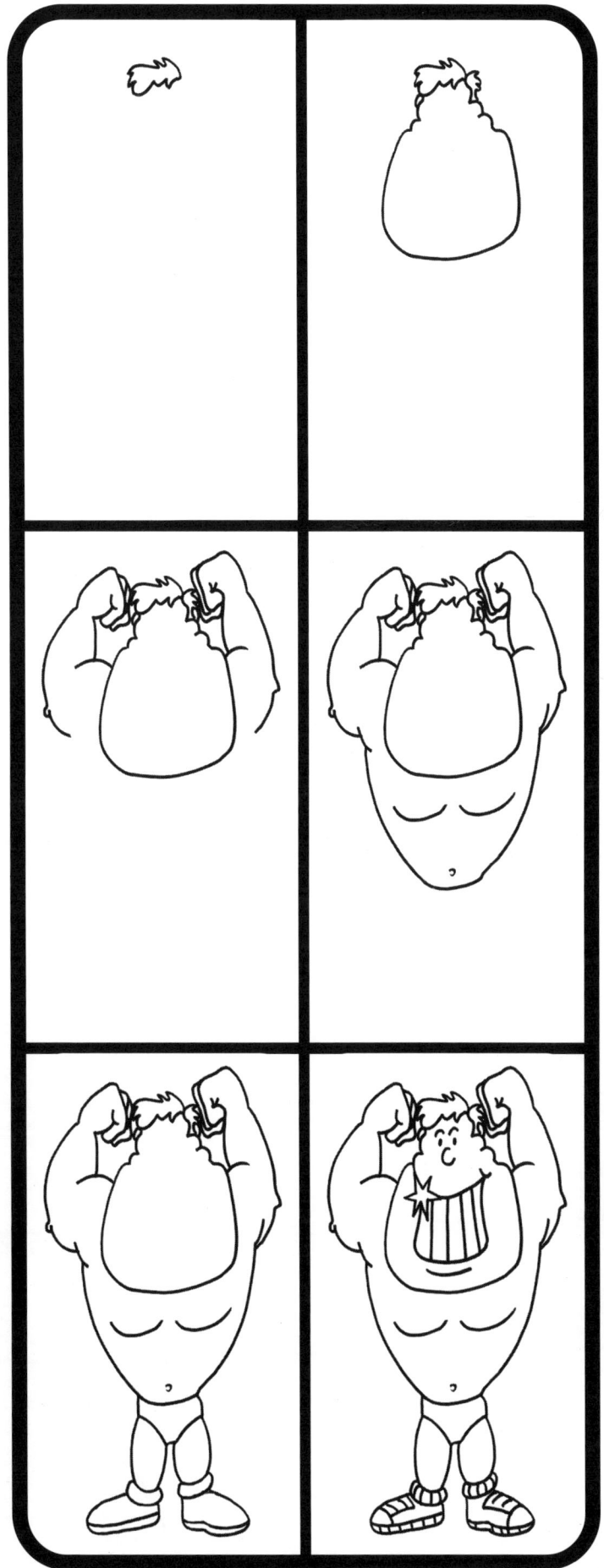

Super Lady   Jaws

Super Gloo

Princess Mighty

Star Chaser

Rocky Hunter

Super Power

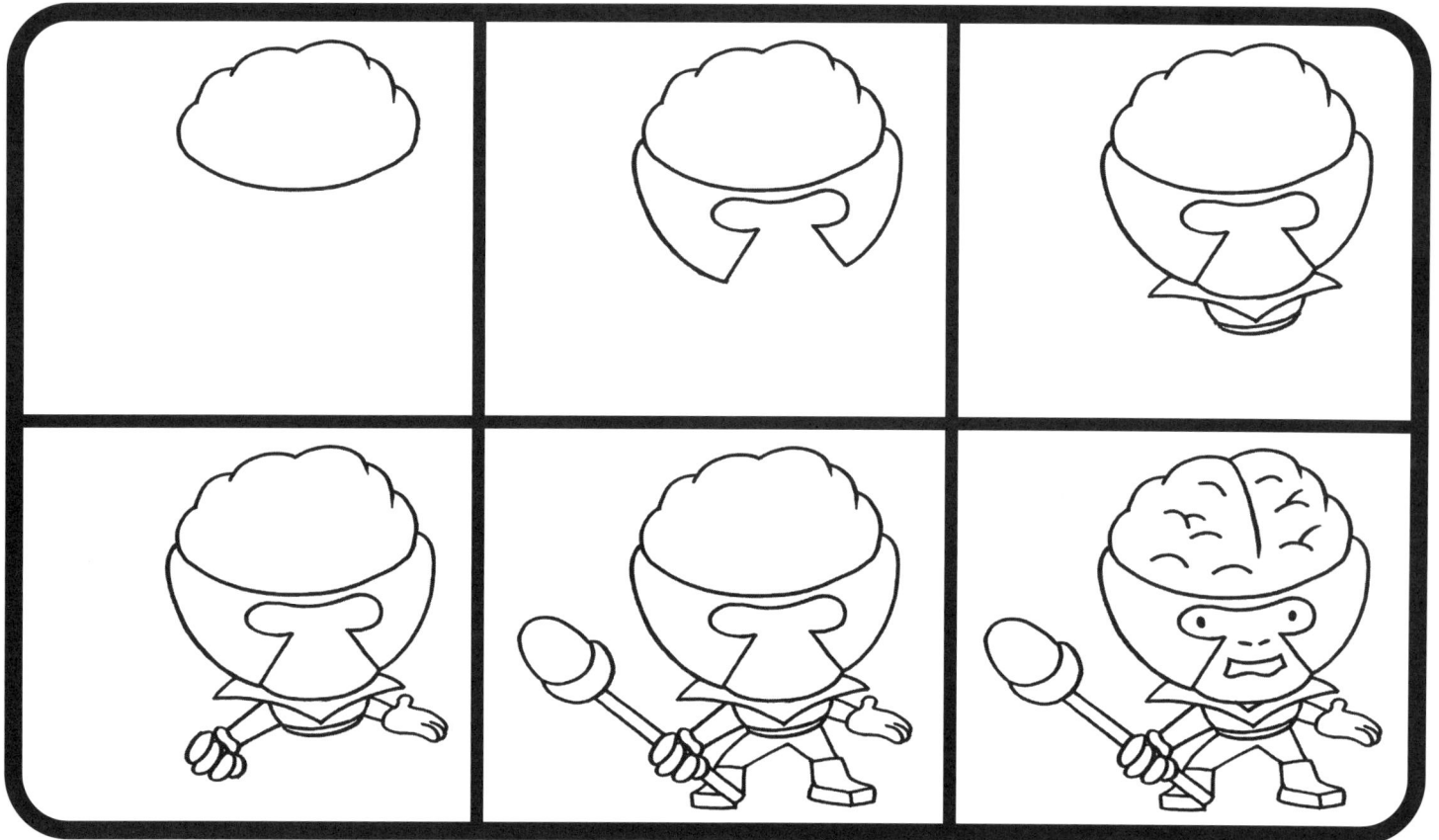

Android

Super Silly-us

Kongo

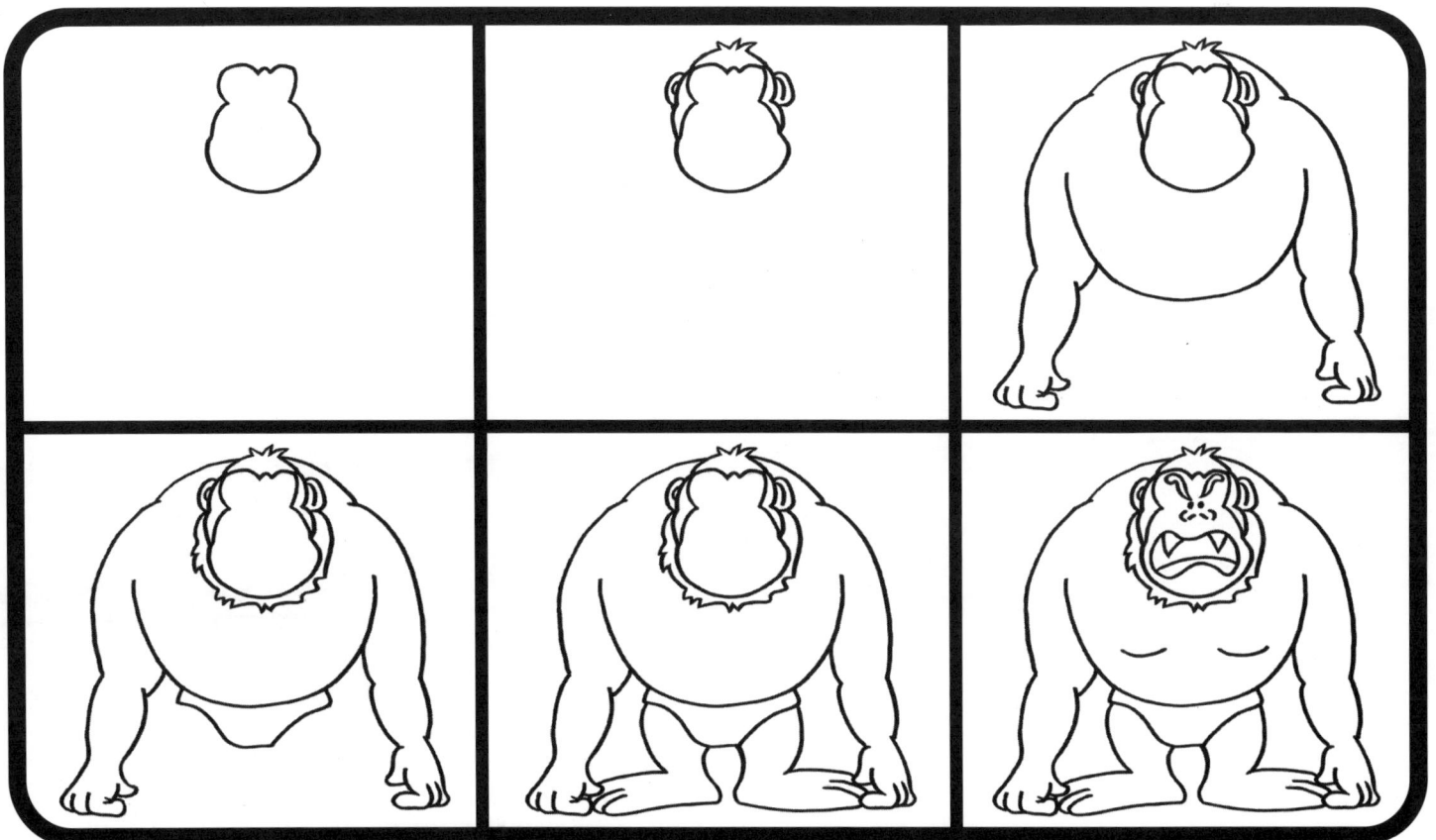

Star Skater

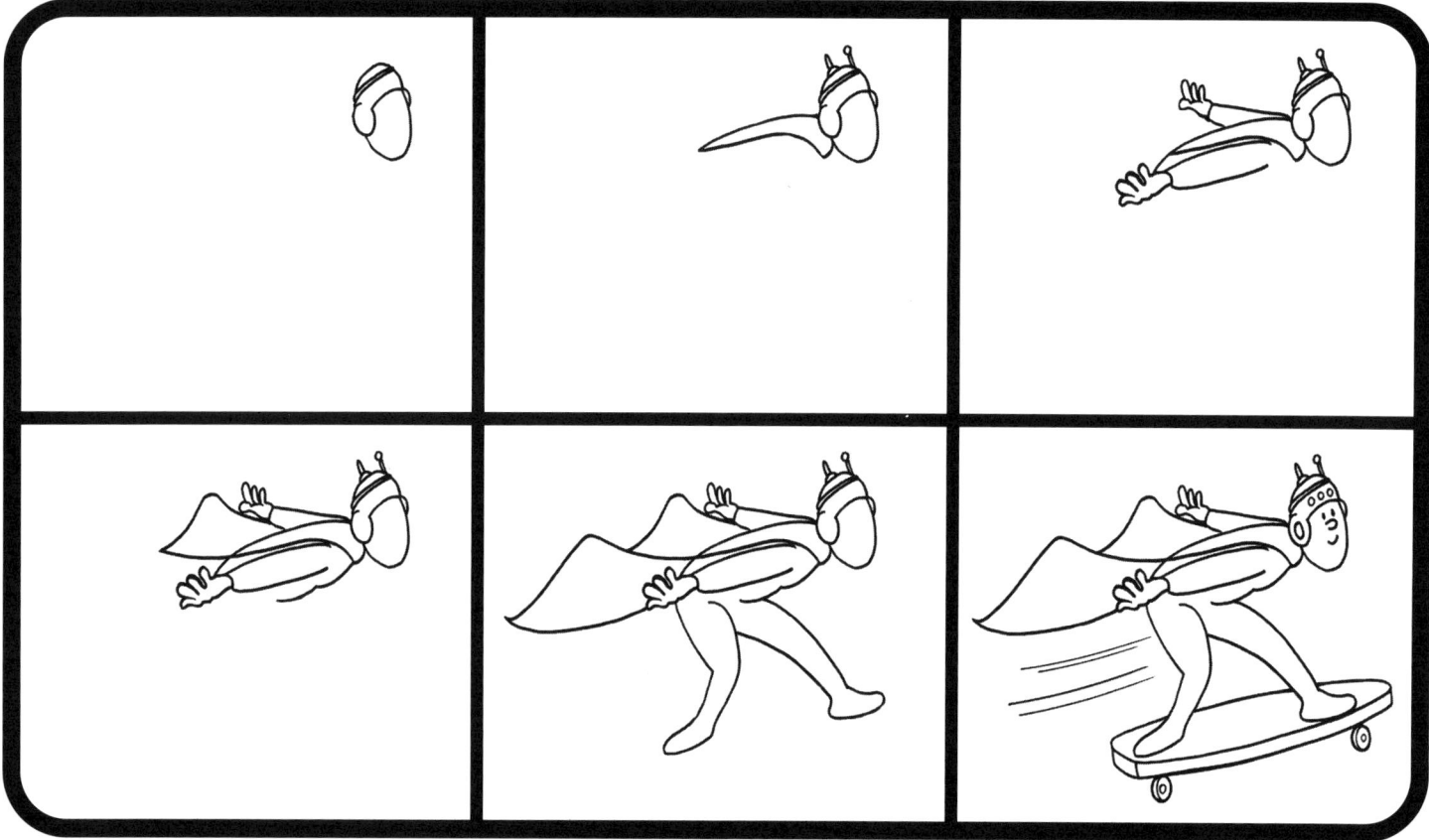

Arachnia

Layzar

Super Swooper

Super Nan

Barbarus

Super Flyer

Space Lancer

 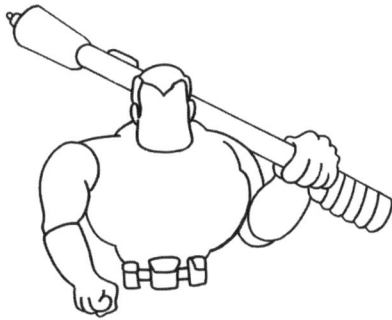

Super Spy

Goliath

Sitting Bull

Super Strongman

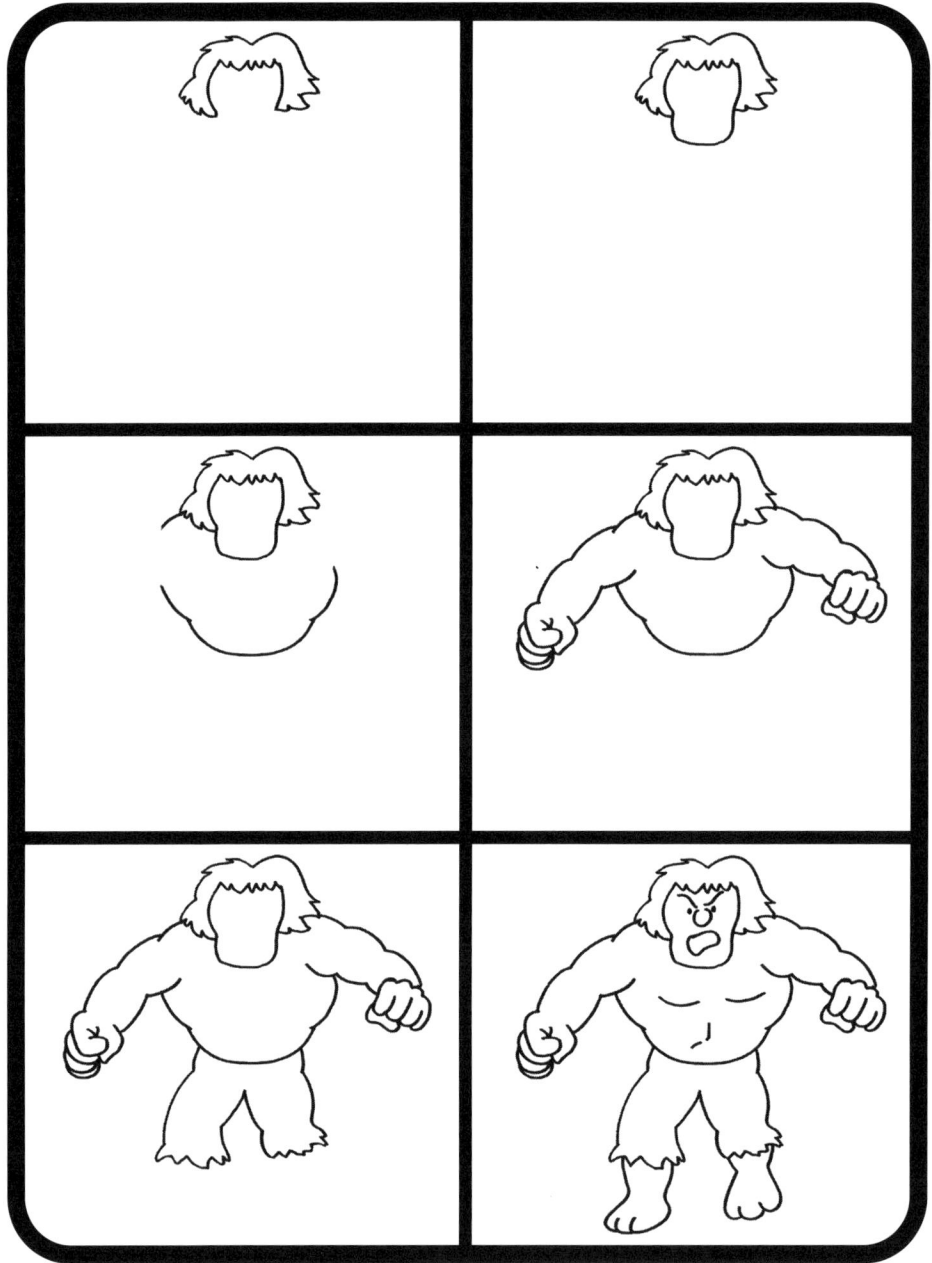

Space Saver

Iron Man

Super Boy

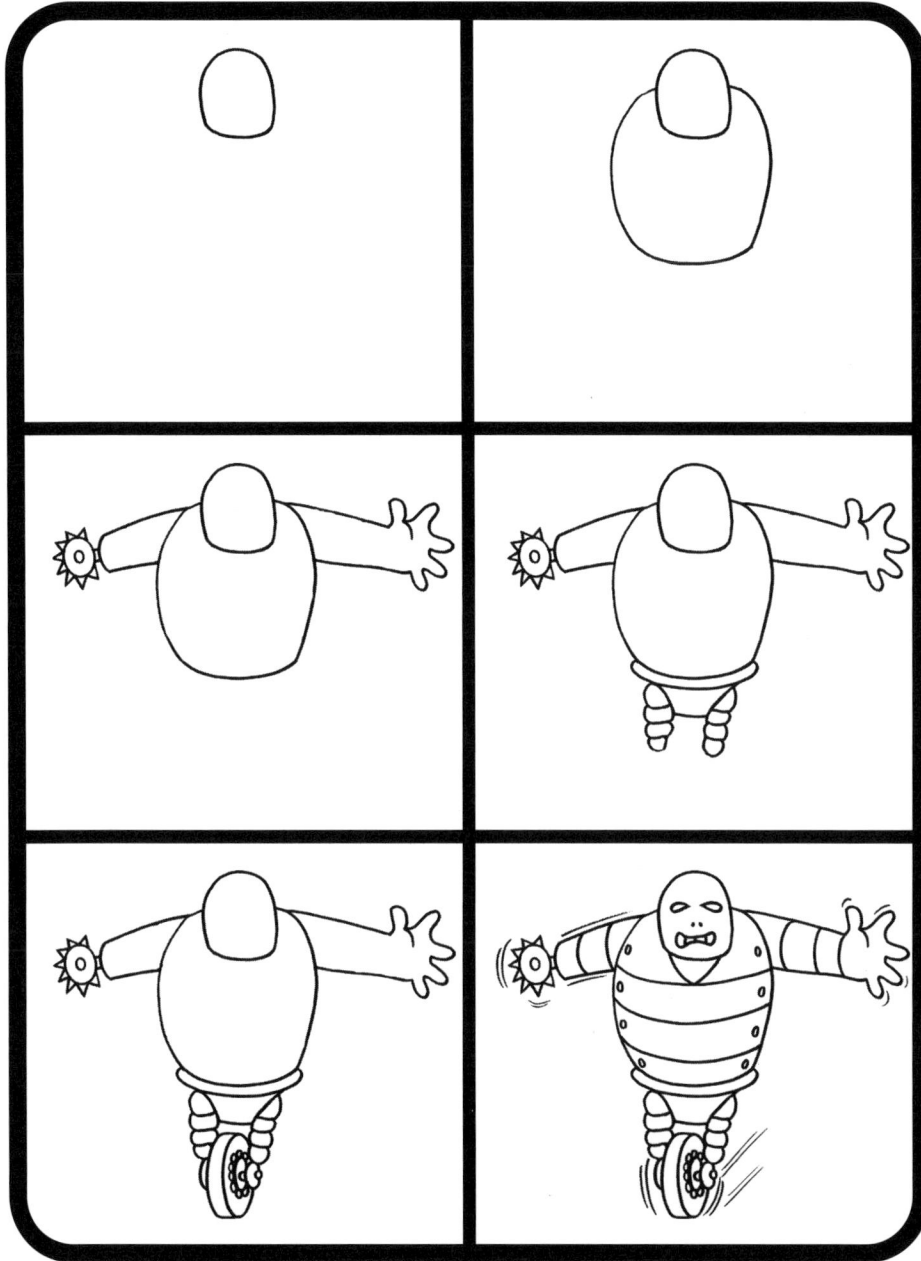

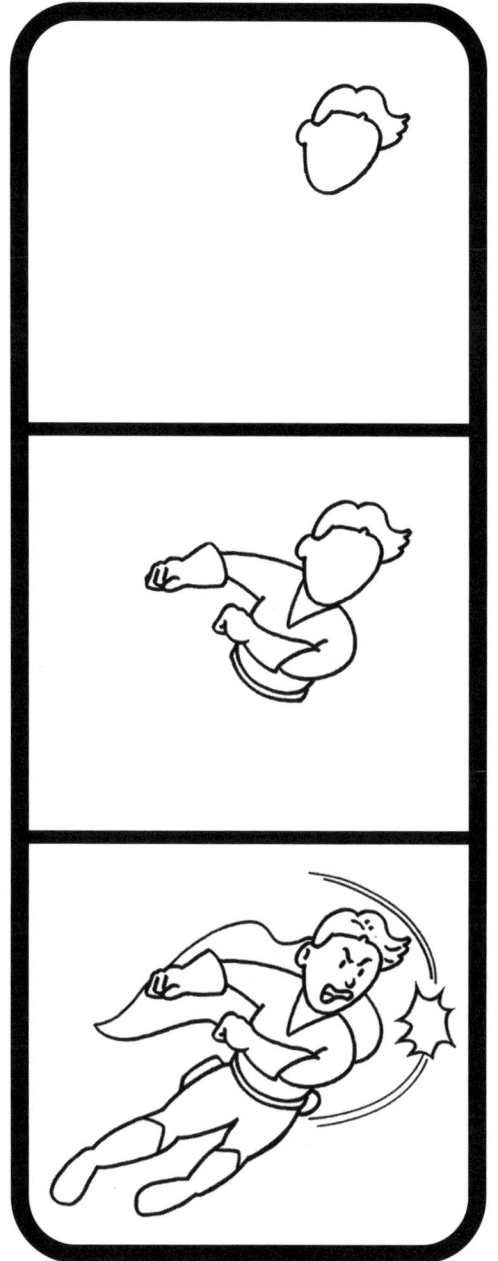

Super Woof

Super Bunny

Big Beard

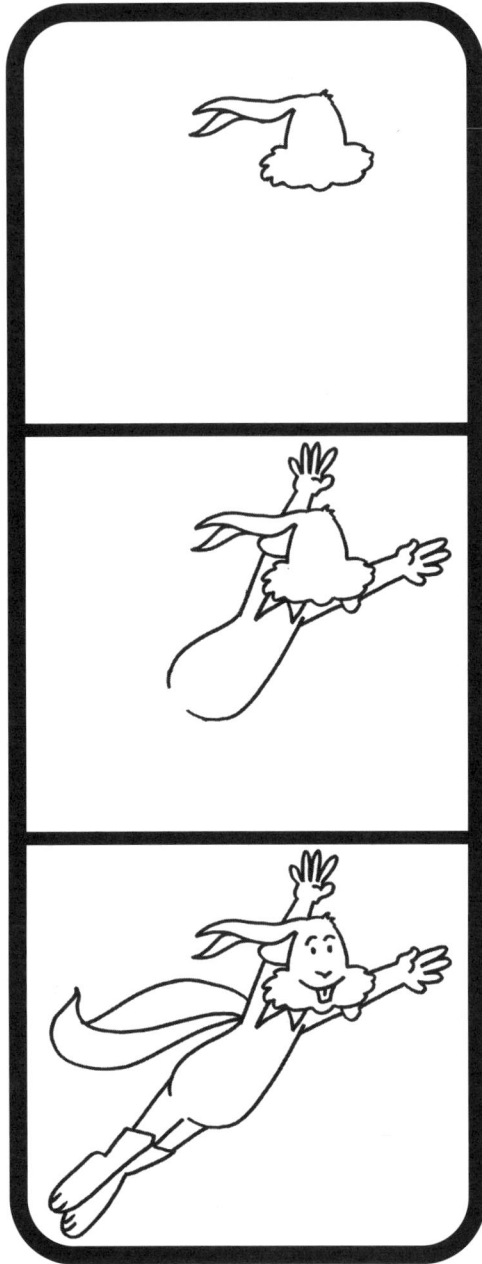
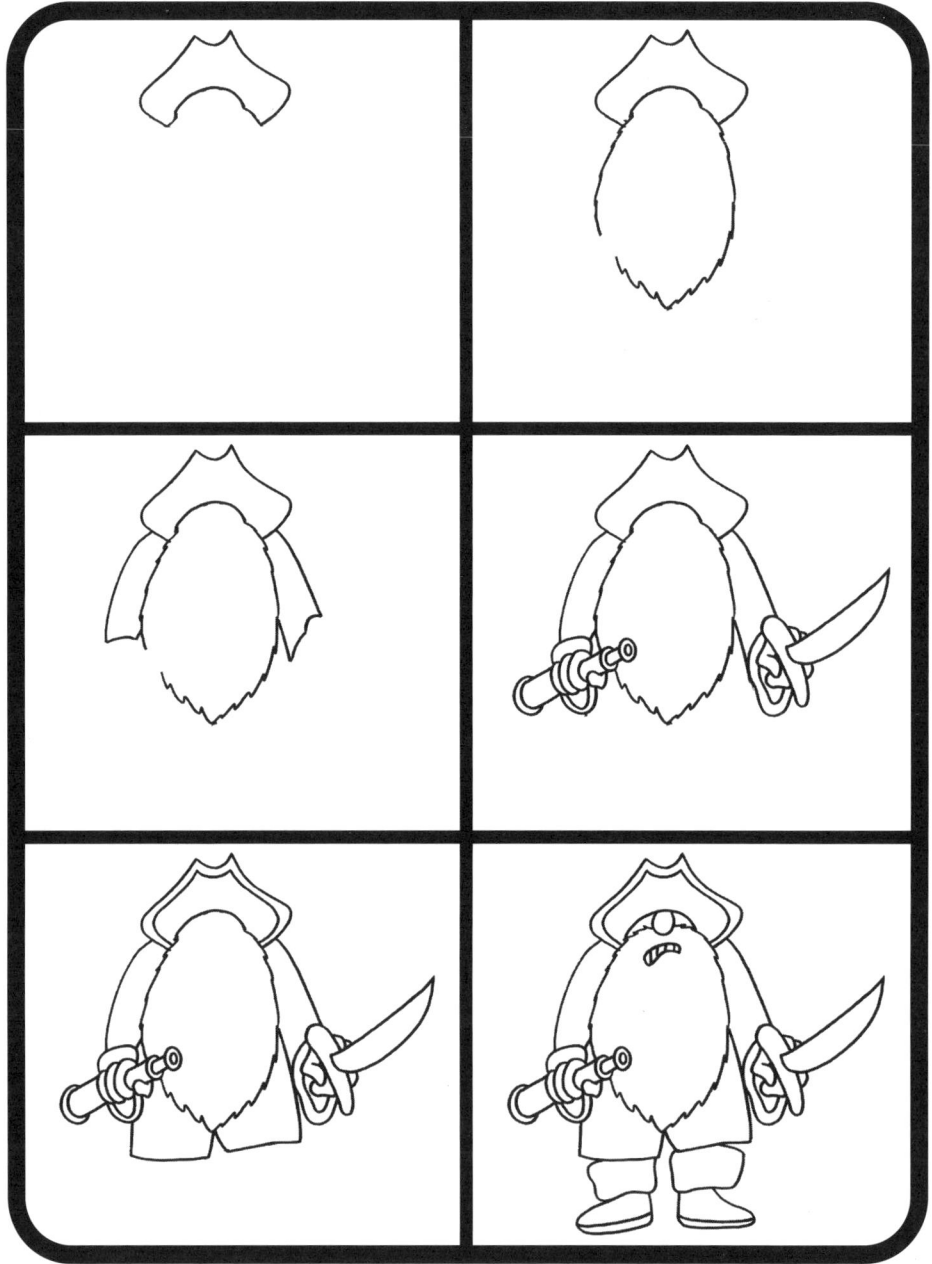

Mighty Mog